PHILIP
THE
TIGER

TALKING FINGERS

DEDICATION

This book is dedicated to the Almighty God, the maker, and finisher of my fate.

CONTENTS

ACKNOWLEDGMENTS

My foremost appreciation goes to the Almighty God for making today a reality, may his name forever be praised. I sincerely appreciate my partner for his love and care about this work. making it easier for me to write in my leisure time. **I LOVE YOU SO MUCH**

1 <u>THE MOTIVATORS</u>

On a Sunday evening, Philip and his parents were watching a tv series, there was a group of young children performing on the stage. The performance was amazing so much, that it caught Philip's attention, jumping and smiling.

Philip turned to his parents, in his nice voice, and said I would like to learn how to dance. Philip's mother replied him with a smile, and his father nodded in approval of his request. He asked his mum if she was a good dancer in her prime but his dad responded, your mum was one of the best dancers in college. She had performed at different events in college and earned an award. Philip's mum happily asked, should I show you a few moves, son? Yes, mum replied Philip. Philip's mum got up from where she sat and turned her back. She took afoot forward with her waist bent while Philip was waiting to witness his mum performing. She began to shake her waist going to and fro. Philip Clapped his hands while his dad smiled at his wife. Some minutes later, Philip was feeling sleepy, he left his parents for his bedroom.

2 **<u>THE DANCING SCHOOL</u>**

A day after, Philip was registered in a dancing school. Philip on his first day in dancing school walked around the school environment, he was surprised by the faces of the members of the group, whose majority of them weren't encouraging to a new member. The young Philip summoned up courage and was able to make his way through his onlookers.

Sooner, the coach whistled for the group training to begin. Philip among his peer watched carefully to take his first lessons. Some minutes later, the coach whistled. Behold, it is time to demonstrate the lessons learned. Philip got the first two moves right but was wrong with the third move. This leads to jeers among some of the members of the group and is followed by uncontrollable laughter from the coach. Philip felt discouraged by the expression of an attitude toward him by some of the group members, including the coach. The coach concluded with Philip's peers and moved on to another group for their performance. Philip walked down to a corner of the building and sat down moody. No one pays attention to him because another group was performing at the moment. He began to think about what had happened while waiting for his dad to come to pick him. His dad arrives a few minutes later.

3 __THE FATHERLY LOVE__

On their way home, his father noticed Philip is not happy. He asked the young boy what had happened. Philip said I don't think I would be going to the dancing school any longer. The father was surprised, Philip explained what happened and the experience he had at the school. His father encouraged him and that brought a smile to his face.

A few kilometers away from home, Philip sees a group of young boys playing basketball on a small court. The joy on the face of these young boys made Philip fall in love with the game. The young Philip called his dad's attention pointing at the court saying, dad, I want to join them. His dad stopped to pay attention to him, looking in the direction Philip was pointing. He saw a group of young children and other two adults. Philip and his dad walked down to the court. Philip's dad greeted the two men and then asked who is in charge, the man with half-whitening beards replied, I'm in charge, how do I help you, man? Philip's dad said, my kid wants to join your team. The other man who seems to be in his 30s busted into laughter, pointing at Philip ridiculously. The half whitening hair man ordered one of the boys to bring the ball. He asks the small boy to throw the ball to Philip to catch, the small boy did but Philip could not grip the ball. He fell to the ground due to the force of the ball. The two men and some of the group of boys laughed at him. Philip's father got angry but controlled his emotions and grab Philip's hands from the ground he lay. They left the court and continued their journey home.

At home, Philip's mum welcomes her son and husband. She noticed her son was unhappy and she asked Philip what happened to him. Philip tried to open his mouth to narrate his unlucky day adventure to his mother, but his father cuts in and explained all that happened to his mother. Philip's mum drew him closer and crease his hair. She made him smile and hurried him to go take his bath because she had prepared a delicious meal.

Philip the tiger

4 <u>**THE PUBLIC HOLIDAY**</u>

It's a public holiday, Philip's dad was sitting outside his home enjoying the cool weather with his son Philip. A few meters from there, there were a group of teenagers playing football in the open space. Philip's father who is a football lover admired a young talent who has been using some amazing tricks on his opponents. Philip's eyes were also focused on them, but was amazed at the way the spectators were applauding the young Messi. He is being motivated by the boy that plays like Messi. He said to his dad, Can I also play football? Yes of course answered his dad. Philip curiously asked how? His father said I will enroll you in a football academy, you will learn the basics of football and you will be trained to become a professional like Messi and Ronaldo. Philip had heard of these great players from many adult discussions, and each time his dad discuss football with his friend, they also talk about them; so he knew they are great indeed.

Later in the day, Philip and his dad visit a football Academy that wasn't far from their home. Philip had been registered after some minutes of discussion and agreement between his dad and the man in charge of enrollment. He was told to begin training the following day.

Philip the tiger

5 <u>THE FOOTBALL ACADEMY</u>

The day breaks, Philip is set to go to the football Academy with his dad who is going to work but Philip is still on holiday in school. They left home and on getting to the Academy entrance, they met a lot of people who had brought their children for training before going to their various destinations just like Philip's dad. Philip is surprised to see a lot of young boys because it is his first time training in a football academy. His dad waved at him and zoom off while Philip join the group of young boys walking into the academy.

Inside the dressing room, they all put on their various kits and set for the training ground where the coach and other trainers await them. The training started with soft jogging for short distances and another training followed. Philip continues to train with the group and increase his football skills. Philip continues to improve to the extent that whenever he scored in the group training match, his teammates rally around him to celebrate him. A few of the trainer sees him as a future football star but the coach thinks otherwise. While the training section was going on, the Academy received an invitation to participate in a football tournament, this news was nice to the hearing of Philip and his teammates. They were all advised to put in their best in every section of the training, to guarantee their chances of playing in the tournament. They all left for their various homes at the end of the training happily.

6 <u>DAY OF THE TOURNAMENT</u>

It is the matchday of the tournament, Philip has arrived at the Academy before the scheduled time for their departure for the match venue, he is so eager to play and showcase his talent as the best player on his team. He practiced on his own while waiting for the arrival of his teammates. Some minutes later, the group has all arrived and they left the academy for the match venue as it had already been scheduled.

At the venue, the two teams make their way out of the dressing room for the pitch after the two teams' starting lineup had been made known to all. A few minutes later, the referee blows his whistle for the match to begin. Philip who plays as his team striker, with the jersey number 9 at his back charge his opponent, wins the ball and advances to the opposition half. He is faced with four defenders at the opposition half, he tried to look for a teammate to pass the ball to, but there was no one to pass the ball. He ended up losing the ball, this caused a loud murmuring from the coach. It is just 15mins played so far, the referee blows his whistle signaling to the touchline for a substitute. Behold, Philip is being replaced. Philip unhappily left the pitch, he couldn't believe he had been substituted so soon. He wondered if losing the ball to his opponent in a tight angle like that warrants his early substitute. He felt dissatisfied with the lack of trust shown by his coach. The first half of the game had been concluded after 45mins of a goalless draw. The players returned to the dressing room with their team for the break. The coach blamed Philip for not capitalizing on the error committed by his opponent and stated it has the reason for his substitute. Philip could not utter a word even though he knew the angle was against him. The halftime break is over, the two teams are back on the pitch for the second half of the game while Philip is seated at the edge of the substitute bench thinking about the coach's remarks on his performance. The match ended one-nil in favor of their opponent.

At home, Philip told his dad what had happened in the day's match. His dad felt sorry for him and encouraged him to work harder on the next match.

7 <u>LACK OF TRUST</u>

It is matchday two, Philip had arrived earlier at the Academy for the second time. He carried out a few training sections on his own. A few hours later, the other members of the team with the training crew have completely assembled. They were driven to the match venue with the Academy bus. After a brief discussion among the team members in the dressing room, the coach made the starting lineup known to them all. Philip is surprised, he isn't on the list. Although he is included on the substitute list, he is shocked by the decision of the coach to bench him for such a crucial match, which he had prepared for. The match began some minutes later, Philip watches in the dugout hoping his time to play will come. The first half ended in the advantage of their opponent, leading by a goal to nil.

The teams set out for the second half from the dressing room after various tactical discussions. The match begins with the pass from Philip's team at the center point of the pitch. Philip was waiting to be a sub in the match. To his surprise, it's a two-nil lead for their opponent. He feels hurt watching from the subs bench. He looks in the direction of the coach who was also surprised, he couldn't believe his team conceded so early in the second half of the match. The coach signal to one of his crew, the one who has the tactical map in his hand. Philip in his mind believes it is time for him to be a sub for a teammate but to his greatest surprise, the coach signals to another teammate of his to get ready to go in as a substitute. Philip was so furious but waited to hear from his coach. After the substitution, the match continues in the same fashion his team has been playing. The coach was standing at the touchline giving instructions, but the score remained two-nil in the advantage of their opponent.

It is 80mins of time played, Philip was so emotional that he didn't know when tears dropped from his eyes, which he met with his soft palm. He felt so sad for the lack of trust shown by his coach to him. It is over, the referee blows his whistle. The team knew they are out of the tournament, losing two games out of three group games match but they have a final group stage match the next day.

Philip had gotten home, his dad isn't back from his office. He was welcomed by his mum but the sadness in his eyes could not be hidden. His mum asked him what is wrong with him this time, he explained what had happened to his mum. She drew him closer to herself and made him sit on her lap. She told him not to worry anymore, that her friend's son plays hockey. She believes he would have a better experience over there. This brings a change in his mood. Philip is interested in knowing more about hockey. His mum promised to take him to where he would be trained this time. This was nice to his hearing. He smiled at his mum to show how appreciative it sounds to him.

8 <u>**THE MOCKERS**</u>

It is a new day, Philip's dad has left home for his job. Philip and his mum are getting ready to go out together as promised. Philip asked his mum if his dad knew he isn't going to the football Academy again, his mother replied, don't worry dear, I have informed your dad about everything that you had experienced at the Academy and I have informed him about our visitation to the hockey training academy today. Philip is happy his dad is in support of him not continuing at the football Academy. He hurried to get himself prepared for today's adventure in hockey training school. Philip and his mum left home for the hockey training Center. Philip's mum met the school representative and discuss other terms of the enrollment. Philip had been registered and he decided to see the Academy environment. Philip saw a group of boys coming, they are taller and huge in their physical appearance. They look so young just like Philip but with a bigger physique, they are 18 in number. Behind them comes a man who seems to be in his 40s. The boys have their eyes on Philip who keeps staring at them. One of them said in a louder voice, who is this small boy here? They have reached where Philip was standing looking sad on hearing the boy's remarks about him. Philip summoned his courage and speak in his timid voice, hello guys, my name is Phillip, am here to join your team. They all busted into laughter, including the coach. The coach said to Philip, "small boy!" how do you compete for a spot in the team with your elder brothers who are 16 in number for a starting spot? Go home and enjoy your chips with your parent. The boys and their coach walk on while Philip was left in shock. Philip tried to hide his worry this time around from his mother. He went to her where she was waiting for him, putting on a fake smile. They left the training Center for their home.

9 <u>THE HOPE</u>

Later in the day, Philip's friend who lives in the neighborhood came to play with his friend, Philip. Philip is happy to see his friend and share his pain with him. His friend felt his pain and comforted him. Then his friend tells him about his martial arts school which he joined not quite long. He told him what he has learned to do and how encouraging the school instructors are. This good news lifted Philip from his sit, he begged his friend to show him some moves, which he did. He said to his friend, what is the name of your martial art school? The boy said ASPIRE MARTIAL ARTS. Philip couldn't hold on to breaking the good news to his parents. He rushed upstairs shouting Mum! Dad!

On getting upstairs, he met his parents at the door, they were waiting to know what has lightened up his spirit this time. Before they could utter a word, he said mum and dad, I want to join my friend's martial arts school. Simultaneously, martial arts! his parents asked. Philip nodded with a smile on his face. His parents followed him to his friend who was waiting for him while standing and looking in the direction of the stairs.

After a brief talk with Philip and his friend, Philip's dad calls his friend who is the father of Philip's friend. The man asked Philip's dad, to visit the school website aspiremarsd.com for more information.

10 **THE ENCOURAGEMENT**

Philip has been enrolled to ASPIRE MARTIAL ART school. He dressed up to go with his friend to school. He left home, happily waving to his parents.

At the martial arts school, Philip walks happily with his friend, into school. He saw people training with different types of equipment that were accompanied by instructors. He saw some instructors correcting their students in an encouraging manner which put a smile on his face while watching them where he was standing. He felt a touch on his shoulder, he turned to see who it was, it was a man dressed in the costume of martial art which he had seen earlier. The man asked, are you, Philip? He nodded yes I'm. The man smiled at him and grab him by the hand, come with me. The man took Philip to where he dressed him martial art costume of his own. He was so excited to have put on such a costume and then took Philip with Him to the midst of his peers. The man said to them, we have a new member, his name is Philip. They clapped their hands to welcome him. He instructed them to recite the laws and principles of the school to him. Simultaneously, they echoed:

1. Be respectful
2. Use what you learn wisely
3. There is no first attack
4. Seek perfection of character
5. Put forth your best effort
6. Calamity springs from carelessness
7. Makes adjustments according to your opponent
8. Maintain a beginner's heart
9. Be faithful

Philip was taught some basics of martial arts. This increases his love for martial arts.

Philip the tiger

BY BENYA

11 <u>**THE HERO**</u>

Later in the day, Philip was so happy when he got home. He even recites those rules to the hearing of his parents, they were so impressed to see that Philip has finally seen something that impresses him. Philip continues to learn martial arts and improve in strength and self-confidence. But he doesn't get carried away.

On one fateful day, Philip was walking his way to his friend's house. He saw three young boys bullying a young girl in a corner of the neighborhood. He told those boys to let go of the girl, but they tried to bully him. He took an afoot back to go on his way, then he thinks of what he had been taught in his martial arts. He decided to stand against the bully using a few of the moves taught in ASPIRE MARTIAL ART school. He rescues the young girl from the bully.

Fortunately, the parents of the young girl and some other group of people who had been looking for her saw them. They were impressed with the heroic deed of Philip, they praised him by calling him the name PHILIP THE TIGER. His heroic deed soon reaches his parents and his martial arts school.

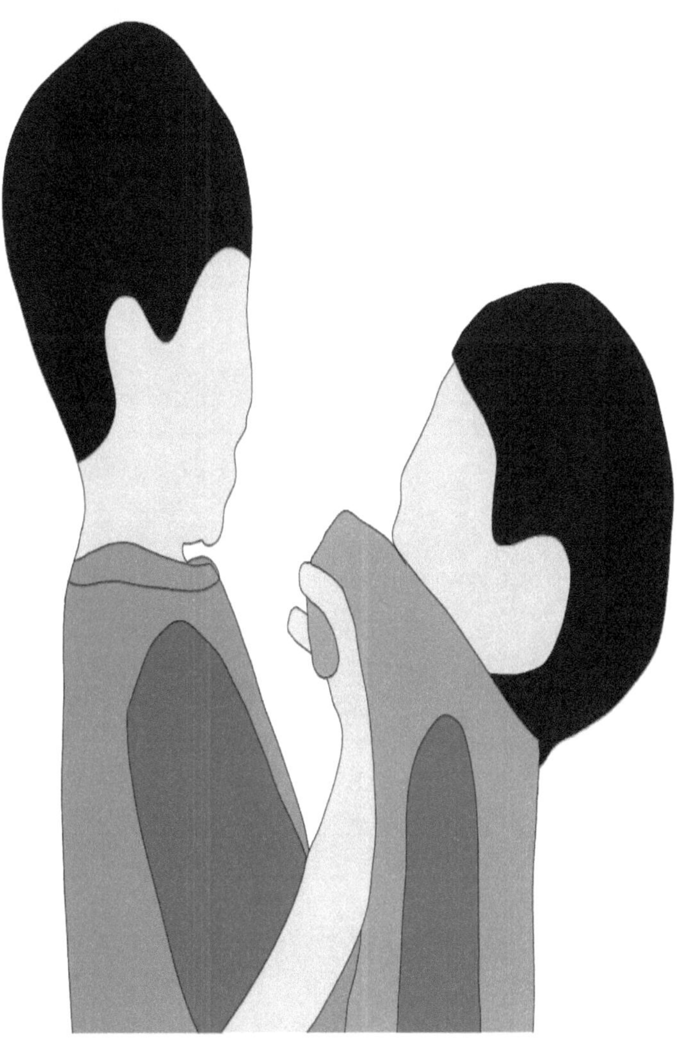

ABOUT THE AUTHOR

I'm TALKING FINGERS the writer of the book 'PHILLIP THE TIGER', which is my first book on Amazon. I have written several printed books which am yet to publish on Amazon. These books include novels like Jilt, Help from Hell, and when I look into your eyes. I also wrote several Christian books which are Christianity and universal values, why Jesus loves you, The judgment day and others.

I have written numerous children's story books that are educative and of moral lessons.

I currently work as a freelancer on Fiverr, Upwork, and Brybe. I love bringing imagination to reality which makes me a good poet.

WATCH OUT FOR ALL THE LISTED BOOKS ON AMAZON SOON

I will be publishing all my previous and ongoing writings here on Amazon.

9 7 9 8 8 3 8 2 2 3 9 1 3